There's a Lion in my Bathroom

THERE'S A LION IN MY BATHROOM

by
Giles Paley-Phillips
Illustrated by Matthew Dawson

REBEL BOOKS LLP

First Published in this format in Great Britain
in 2010 by Rebel Books LLP
OC345244
www.rebelbookspublishing.co.uk

Individual poems Copyright © Giles Paley-Phillips
The moral right of Giles Paley-Phillips to be identified as
the author of this work have been asserted in accordance
with the Copyright, Designs and Patents Act of 1988.

All rights reserved. No part of this publication may be
reproduced, stored in or introduced into a retrieval system , or
transmitted, in any form, or by any means (electronic, mechanical,
photocopying, recording or otherwise) without the prior written
permission of the publisher. Any person who does any unauthorised
act in relation to this publication may be liable to criminal
prosecution and civil claims for damages.

A CIP Catalogue of this book is available from
the British Library.

ISBN 978-0-9565035-2-7

Cover Art and Illustrations Copyright © Matthew Dawson 2010
Cover Design by Matthew Dawson

All of the characters in this book are fictitious, and any resemblance
to actual persons living or dead is purely coincidental.

*A percentage of the proceeds from the sale of this book are being donated
to Leukaemia & Lymphoma Research.*

Leukaemia &
Lymphoma Research
BEATING BLOOD CANCERS

*for Esther, Eda
and Lenny-Uist*

Contents

Snorky the Shrimp, 13

Sleeping, 16

Hallowe'en Night, 17

Sir Robin Hood and Friar Tuck, 18

Timbuktu, 22

Lies, 23

Two Left Feet, 24

Agatha, Tabitha, Maggie and May, 25

Tex, 27

Lion and Tiger Pie, 28

Old Ladies, 29

My Girlfriend, 30

Hairy Armpits, 33

Felicity Jones, 34

There's A Lion In My Bathroom, 37

Sydney Van Dyke, 38

The Boy Who Was Awful At Magic, 40

Colds, 44

Food, 46

The Girl With Springs For Feet, 50

I'd Like To Be, 58

Jonas the Worm, 63

Christmas Trees, 64

The Weather Lady, 65

My Favourite Toy, 66

Football, 70

Nail in My Foot, 72

Dragons, 74

Lonely Tree, 77

Bagshaw, 82

Beddy-byes Land, 83

Chuck the Shark, 88

Coming Apart, 97

Sid the Fly, 98

Snorky the Shrimp

Snorky the shrimp
Had a bad limp,
Which made him cry out loud.

"Oh woe is me,
I can't swim free,
I want to fit in with the crowd."

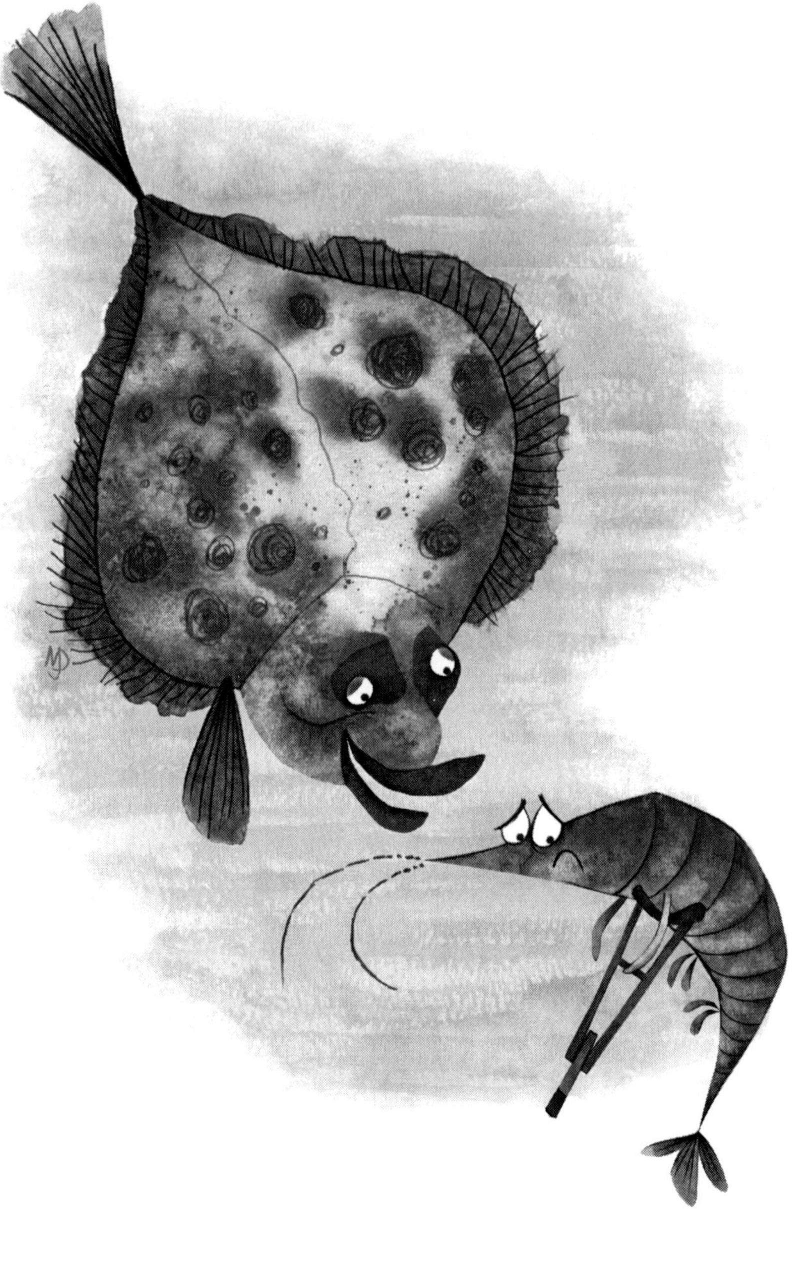

So Hamish the plaice
Wiped the tears from his face,
And gave him a word of advice.

"I've got just one fin,
And I can still swim!
Being different can sometimes be nice."

Sleeping

Sleeping is great, I think you'll agree.
But the best thing about sleeping,
Is the fact that it's free!

Hallowe'en Night

All the trick or treaters ran with fright,
When I opened the door on Hallowe'en night.
I just couldn't figure out what I'd done wrong.
I hadn't even put my costume on!

Sir Robin Hood and Friar Tuck

Sir Robin Hood and Friar Tuck,
They really had the worst of luck.
For at the local archer's show
There was a chance with just one throw,
To win a very handsome prize
A bank account of quite some size.
Tuck placed a bet on fair Sir Robin
(As he was great at arrow lobbing).

With five to one odds on to win,
They could finally quit their life of sin.
Every morning, noon and night
With cunning, skill and hands so sleight,
They had been robbing from the wealthy,
To buy some food to keep them healthy.
But then the fateful day it came,
And poor Sir Robin collapsed in pain.

Whilst practising his winning trick
He drew the bow and with a flick...
The arrow looped into the air,
And struck him through his underwear!
Well I don't need to say much more,
Apart from that he felt quite sore.
So it's back to robbing for a meal
And wearing a codpiece made of steel!

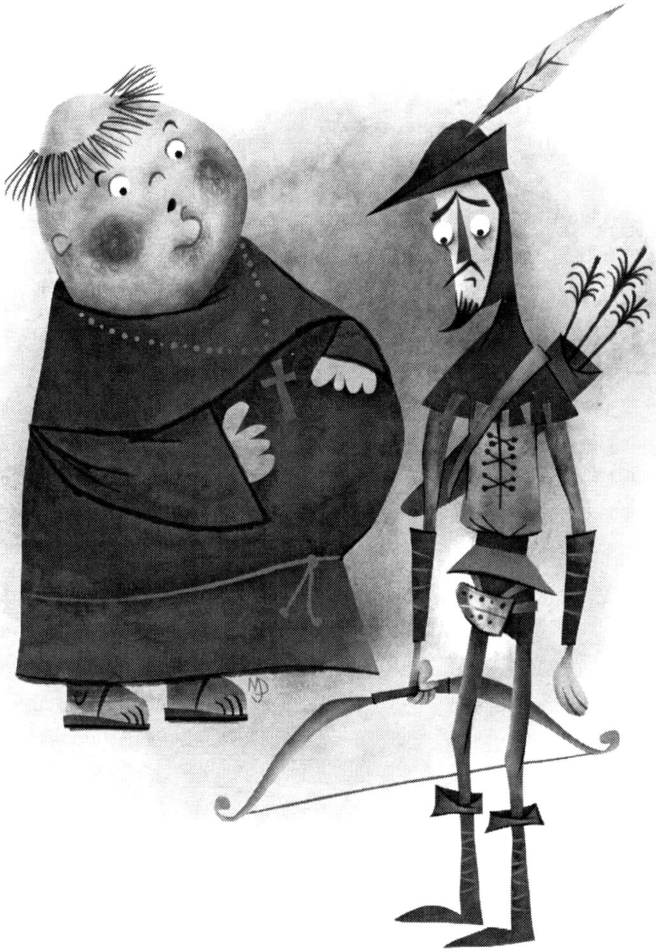

Timbuktu

We used to live in Timbuktu,
But there really wasn't that much to do.
So my mum, my dad, the dog and me,
Moved up the road to Timbukthree!

Lies

I haven't lied

In oh so long.

Except for those times

I got the truth wrong!

Two Left Feet

Having two left feet
Makes walking such a chore,
'Cos going round in circles
Can be an awful bore.

Agatha, Tabitha, Maggie and May

Agatha, Tabitha, Maggie and May,
Built a big rocket and blasted away,
They went to the moon for an overnight stay,
Then came back to earth the very next day.

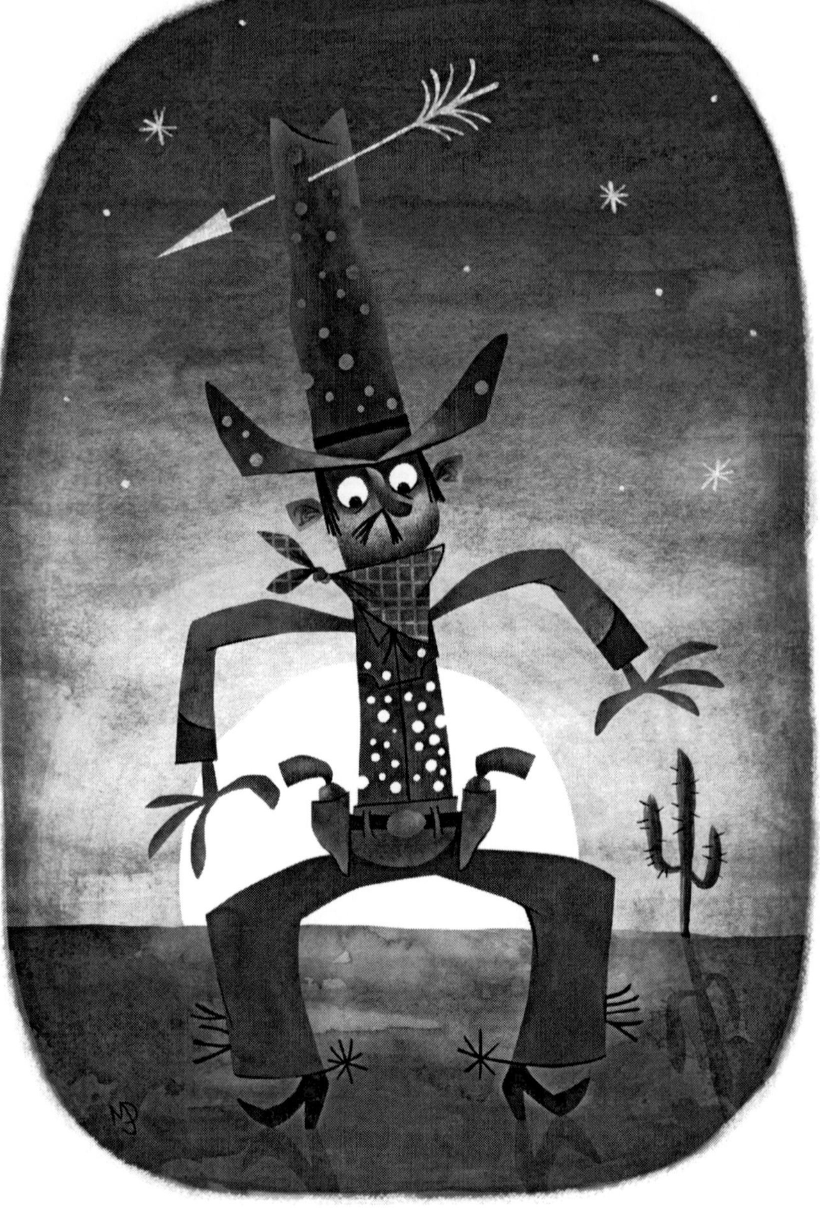

Tex

Tex was the slowest
Gun in the west.
He had more holes in him,
Than an old string vest

Lion and Tiger Pie

Making Lion and Tiger pie,
Is a really tricky thing to do,
Because any attempt to ensnare them,
Can result in a pie made of you!

Old Ladies

The times I think old ladies look weird,
Is when they attempt to grow a big beard.
It always appears to go terribly wrong,
And the few hairs they grow are straggly and long.
But they're very hypnotic as they sway to and fro,
You just can't help but stare when they come out on show.

My Girlfriend

My girlfriend has cardboard hands,
And hair that's made of rubber bands.
Her feet are just two big bricks,
She's not at all like other chicks!

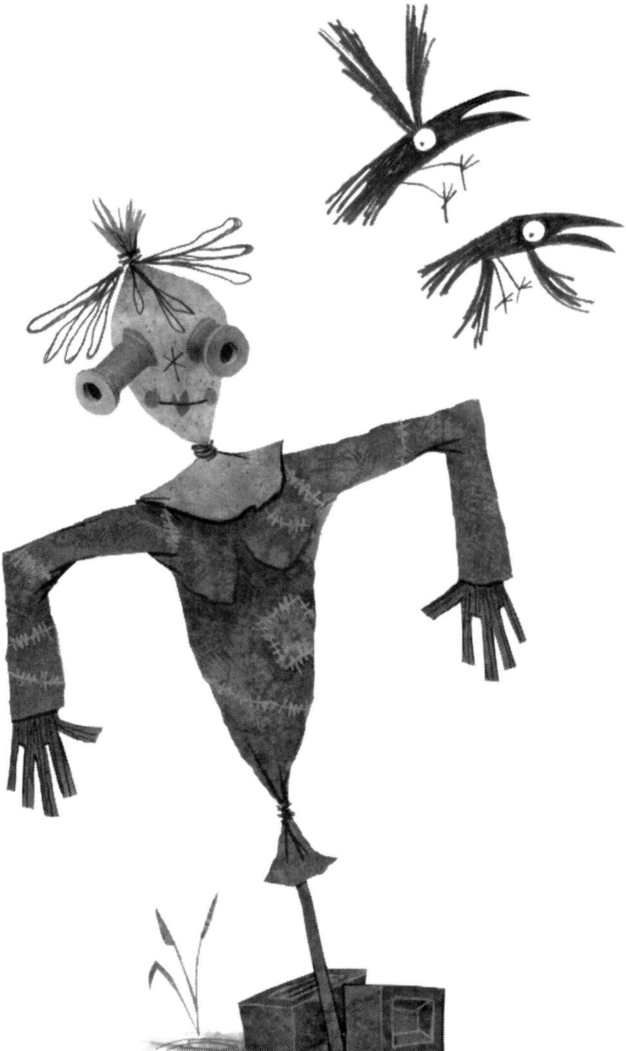

With cotton reel eyes and rancid clothes,
She has the look to ward off crows.
I really love her like no other
So I think I'll make myself another!

Hairy Armpits

My dad has hairy armpits,
Which are great for just one thing:
If you tie them up together,
They make the perfect swing!

Felicity Jones

Felicity Jones loved to talk,
And howl and yell and sing and squawk.
Making noise is what she did,
You never heard a louder kid.

But then one day she lost her voice,
and everyone yelled with rejoice.
"At last our ears can have a break,
And our heads no longer have to ache!"

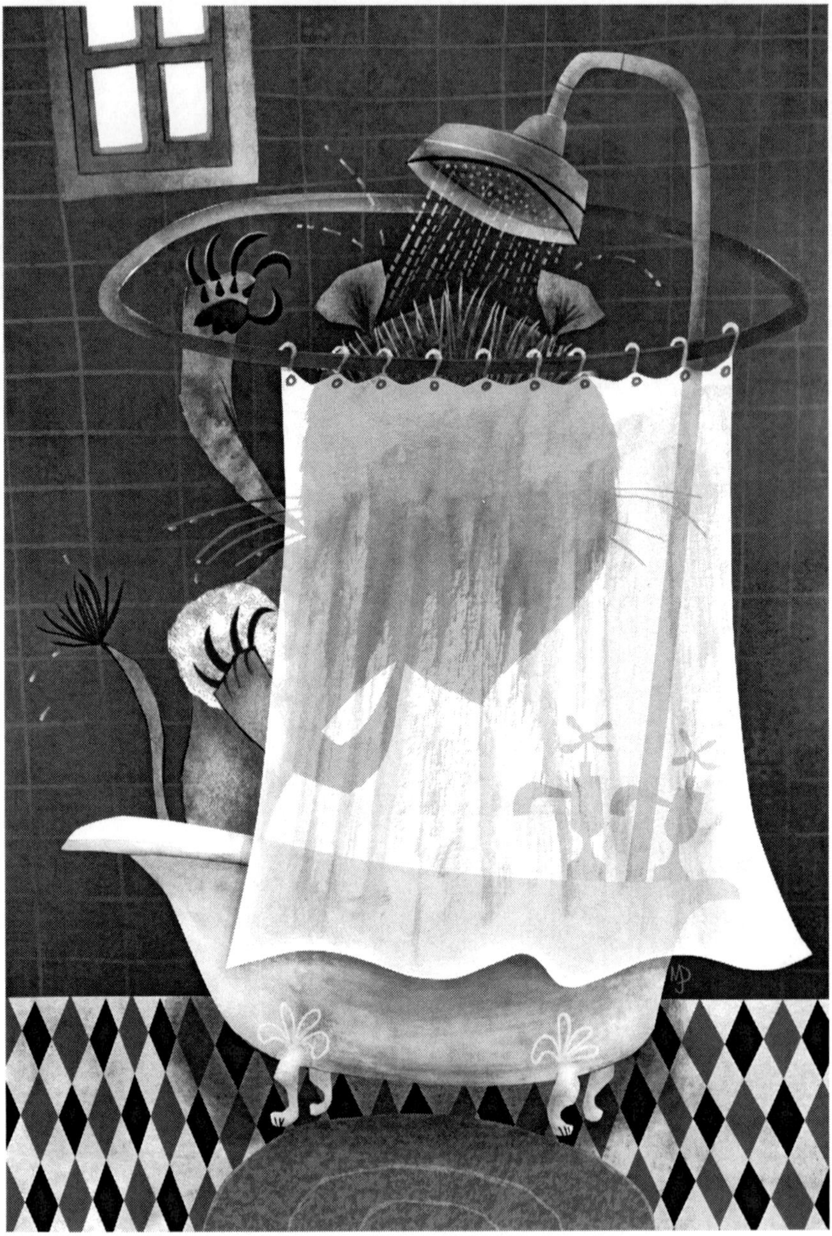

There's A Lion In My Bathroom

There's a lion in my bathroom,
And I don't know what to do,
Because I'm really scared to enter,
But I'm desperate for the loo.

Sydney Van Dyke

Sidney Van Dyke is quite unlike
All the other farmers.
The crops he grows in his fields,
Are all old men's pyjamas

When it comes to harvest time,
   He picks them one by one,
   Washes them in aftershave
   And dries them in the sun.

The Boy Who Was Awful At Magic

There once was a boy who was awful at magic,
whose only trick nearly ended quite tragic.
After months and months perfecting his craft,
He attempted to saw one old lady in half.

As he started to saw he knew something was wrong,

'Whoops', he thought, "there's no safety catch on!"

The old lady screamed at the sight of the blood

As magicians go this boy was a dud.

The audience were in shock and as quiet as a mouse,
The boy had to shout, "Is there a doctor in the house?"
A doctor rushed forth and said, "I shall endeavour
To perform a proper trick, and sew her back together."

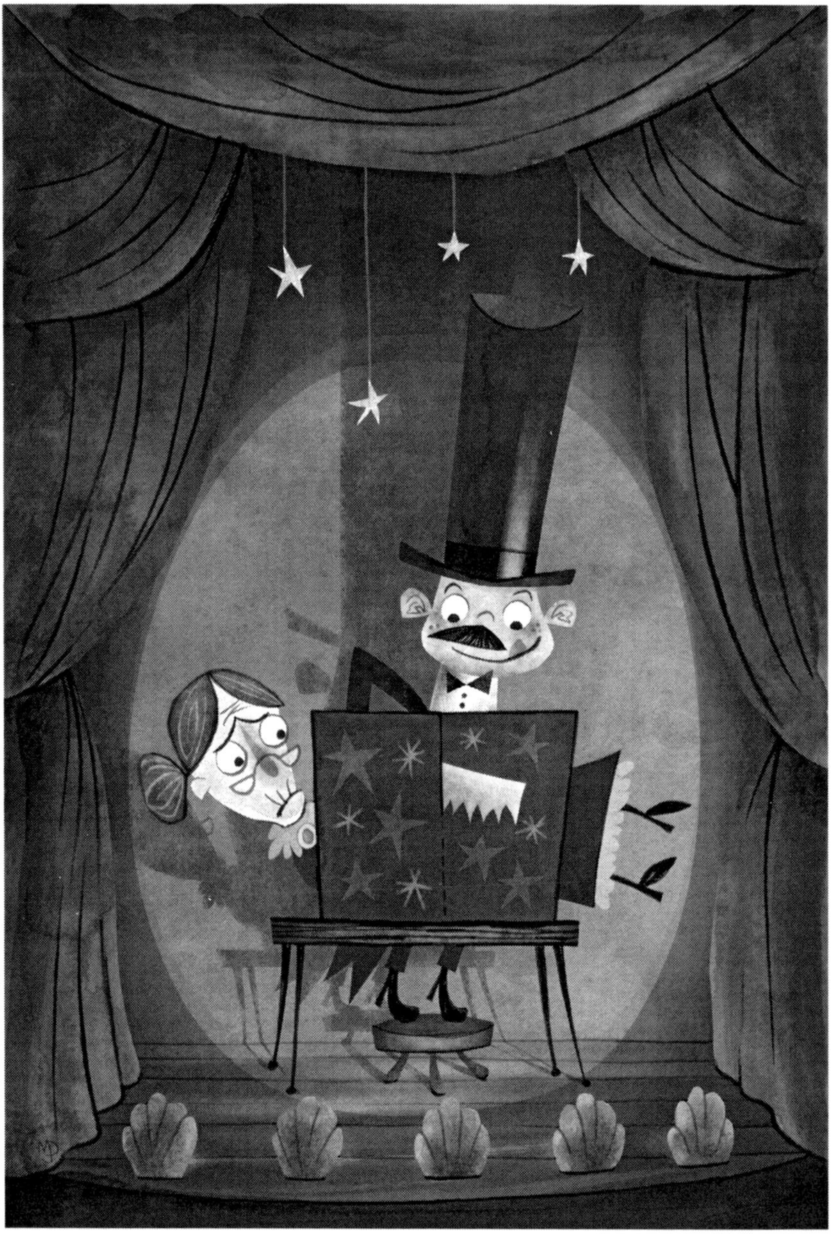

Colds

The other day you caught a cold,
And wouldn't let it go.
So it made you wheeze and cough and sneeze,
Which allowed for snot to flow.

I told you, "Colds don't like being caught,
    They like to roam around free.
      So if you catch a cold again,
      Don't bring it home to me!"

Food

I'll eat bees on top of toast,
I'll eat boots and buckle roast,
I'll eat tins of pickled lice,
I'll eat mud with pan-fried rice.

I'll eat jam made out of fleas,
I'll eat banana-flavoured cheese,
I'll eat spam and crispy ants,
I'll eat my socks and underpants.

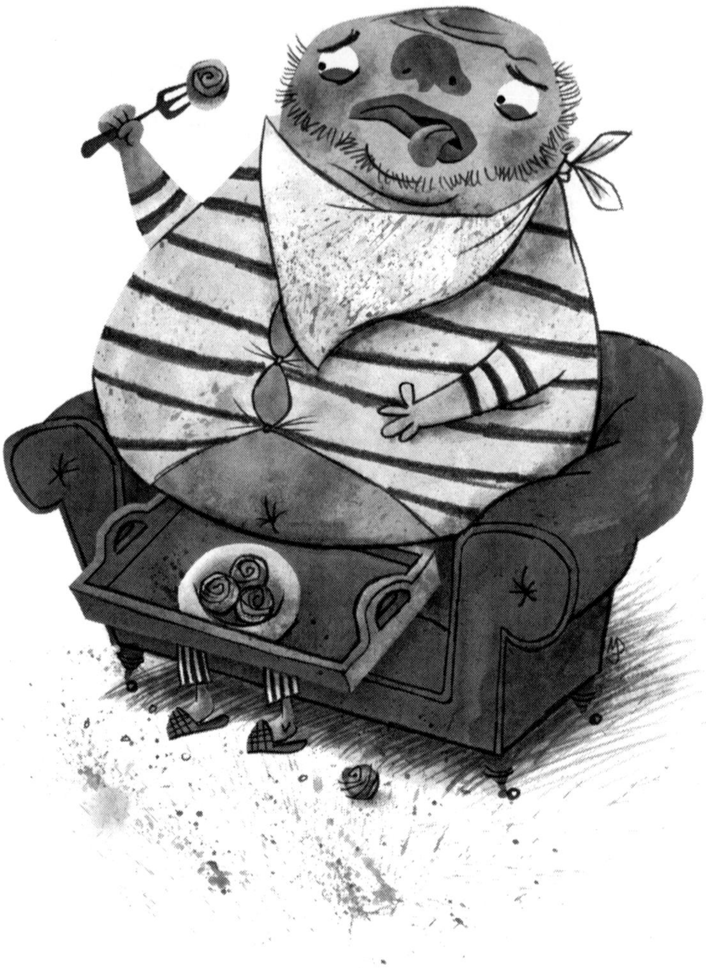

I'll eat pies with cow pats in,
I'll eat just about anything.
But there is one food without a doubt
I'll never eat a Brussel sprout!

The Girl With Springs For Feet

There once was a girl,
Who had springs for feet.
On the day she was born,
Her parents they shrieked

"She can't be ours."

Handing her back to the nurse.

Who replied with a smile,

"This really isn't a curse."

"With feet like these,

I think she is meant,

To become a great champion,

In the long jump event."

And so it came to pass
At the Olympics in Seoul,
Her first jump measured,
Just past the North Pole.

Her second jump was
Even further than that.
She jumped as far
As the moon and back.

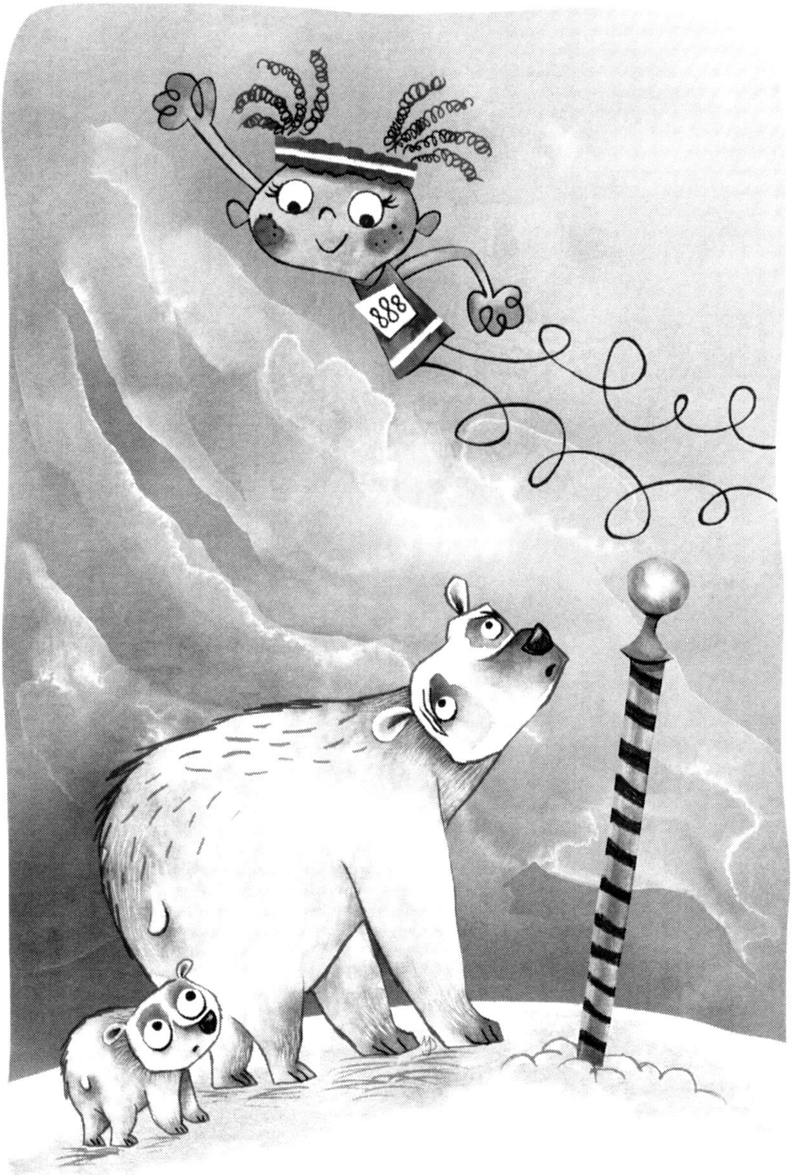
888

All the other athletes
Would have needed wings,
To try and compete
With two feet made of springs.

And this is where,
Our story must end,
On the gold medal rostrum,
With feet that can bend.

I'd like to be...

I'd like to be a lion
And roar really loud.
Or a very tall giraffe
Who can touch a passing cloud.

I'd like to be a cheetah
Running fast across the land.
Or a crab that likes to scuttle
On some lovely golden sand.

I'd like to be a crocodile
With thick and scaly skin,
Making everybody shiver
With my fearsome toothy grin.

I'd like to be an elephant
And have big baggy knees.
Or a cheeky little chimp
Who likes swinging from the trees.

I'd like to be a croaky frog
And sit upon my log.
Or run around, and wag my tail
Like a puppy dog.

I'd like to be a horse
That takes part in many races.
Or a fly that when it looks at us,
Sees lots and lots of faces.

I'd like to be a rattle snake
Slivering on the ground.
Or a mole who likes to poke his nose
Out of a muddy mound.

I'd fly and soar up in the sky
If I were like a hawk.
Or be a noisy parrot
That loves to squeak and squawk.

I'd like to be a bumble bee
And collect up pots of honey.
Or maybe just a grizzly bear
Who wants some in its tummy.

I'd like to be a hippo
And wallow in thick mud.
Or a rhino that when it walks
Makes a noisy thud.

I'd like to be a whale
Swimming deep beneath the sea.
But now I come to think of it
I quite like being me.

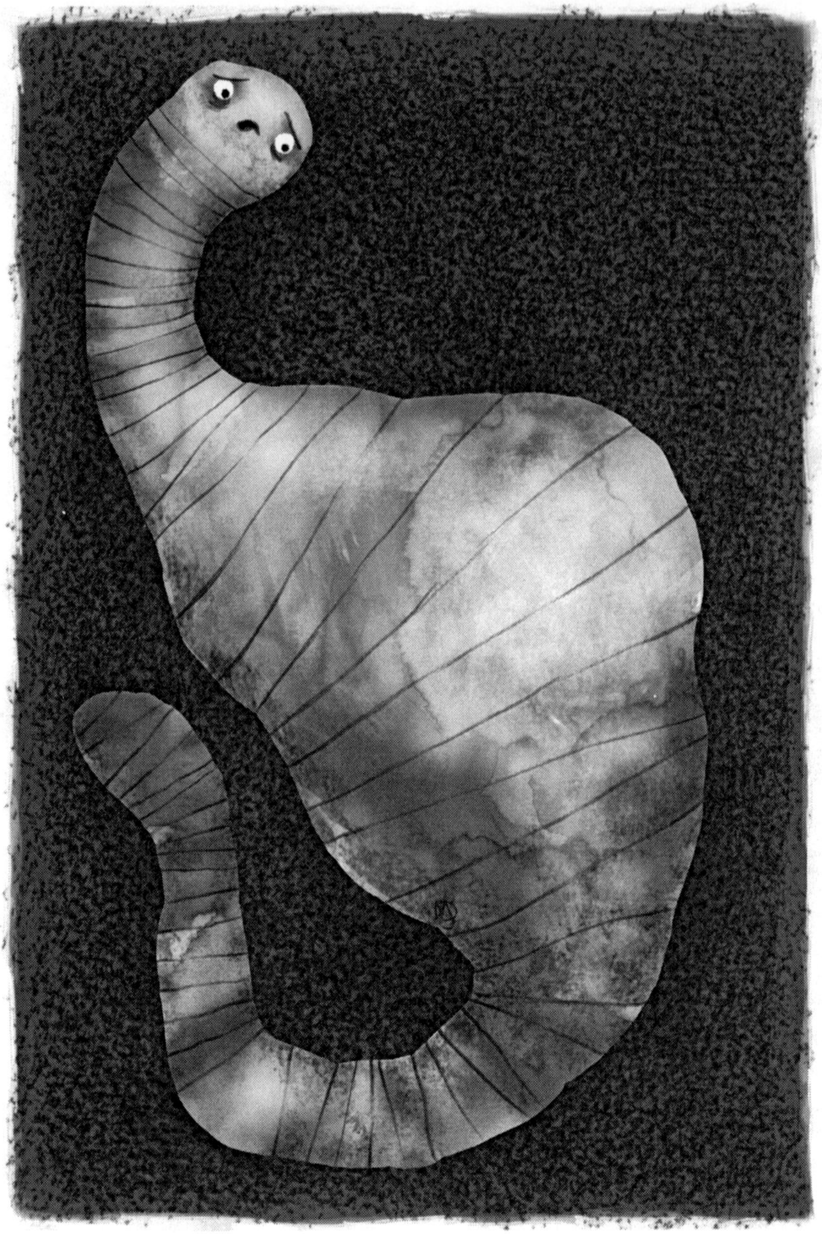

Jonas the Worm

Jonas was an unfortunate worm,
He suffered in life from chronic heartburn.
It had something to do with the soil that he ate,
Not the variety he chose,
More the amount in weight!

Christmas Trees

Christmas trees
Are really quite rude.
Except for Christmas
They stand around nude!

The Weather Lady

My Granny said, "When you look at the skies,
You can usually tell when somebody dies.
'Cos if you look closely when a rain cloud appears,
You'll see that it's filled with Mother Nature's tears."

My Favourite Toy

I had a robot, his name was Roy,
I think he was my favourite toy.
I'd make him do all my chores,
Like ironing clothes and mopping floors.

He'd even tidy up my room,
He was quite nifty with a broom.
My homework was always in on time,
Because Roy did his and then did mine.

When my clothes needed a clean,

He'd put them in the washing machine.

But one day he stopped and I have no doubt,

I had finally worn Roy's batteries out.

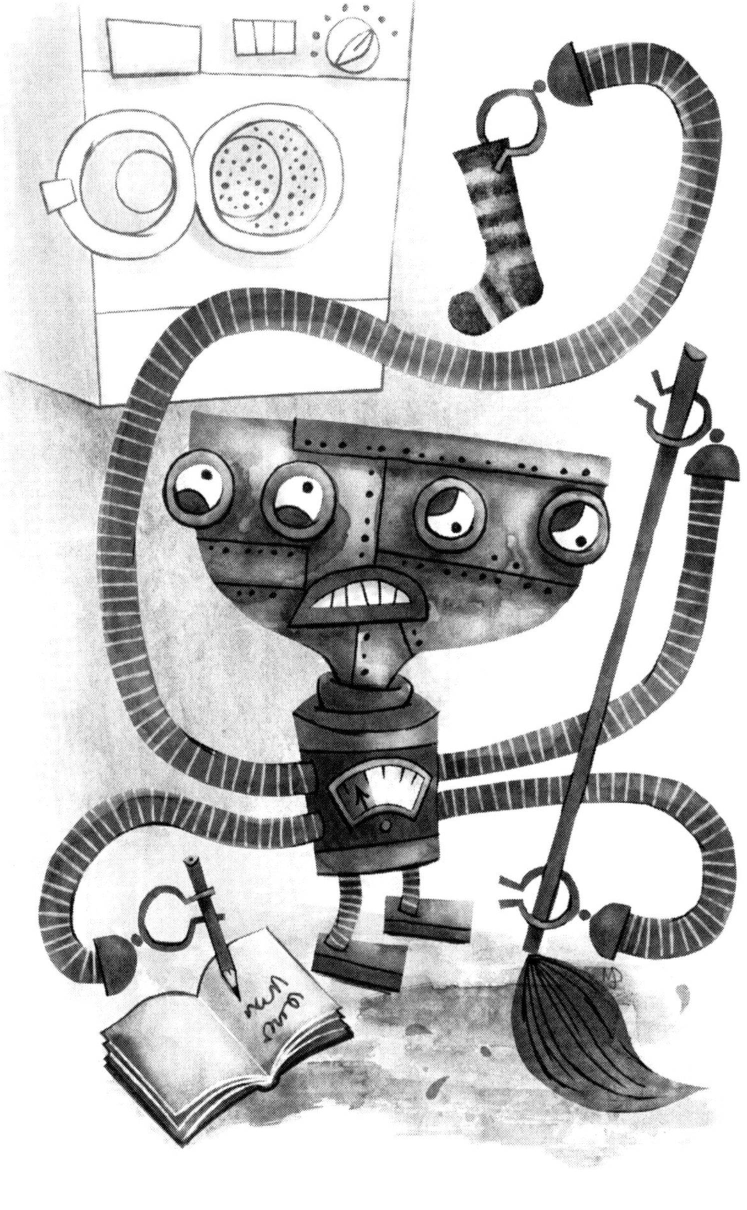

Football

If you want to score a goal,
I have a trick for you.
Just get your favourite football boots,
And smother them in glue.

Then place your foot upon the ball,
    It will stick to the sole.
So when the kick off whistle blows,
    Just hop into the goal.

Nail in My Foot

I've got a nail in my foot,
And I don't know how it got there.
I can't say I've seen it before.

I've got a nail in my foot
Which is really quite annoying
'Cos now I'm attached to the floor

Dragons

Be aware of dragons,
As their very favourite food,
Is a lean and sumptuous child,
Finely chopped and barbecued.

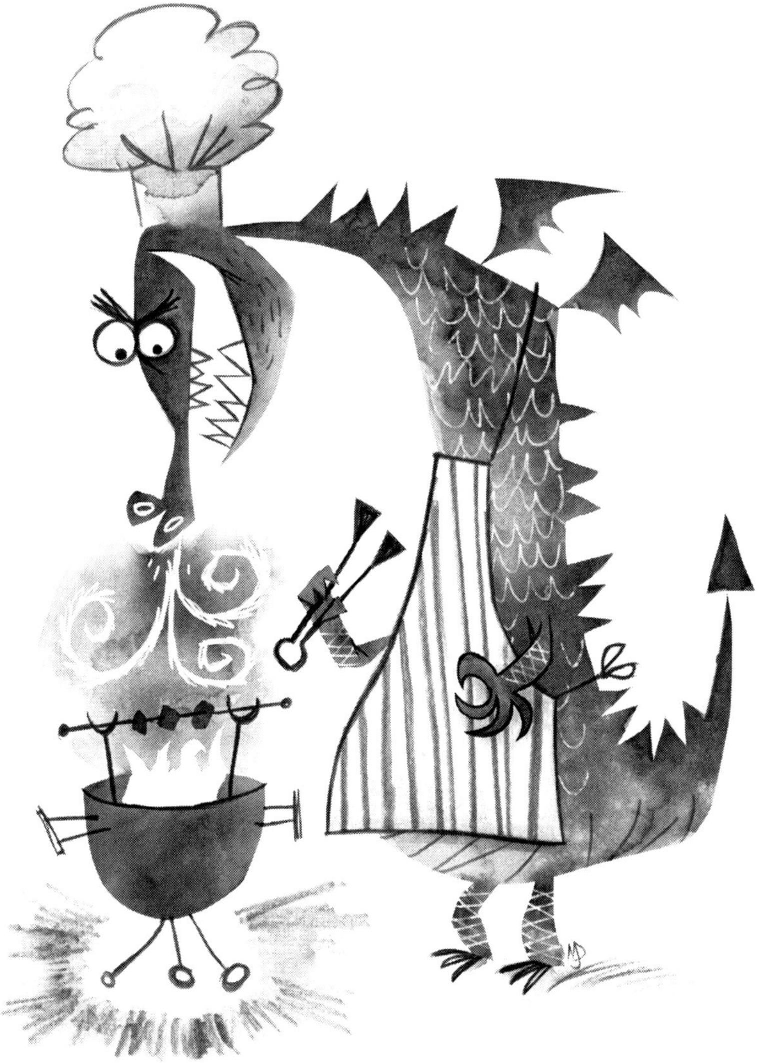

Sometimes as a pudding,

To really fill their tum,

They'll eat a toasted sandwich,

Made of your dad and mum.

Lonely Tree

I passed by a lonely tree,
Who suddenly started speaking to me,
His branches drooped and swayed about,
His leaves were worn and falling out

"I'm tired of feeling lonely," he said,
'I'm tired of being me.
Will someone please cut me down?
So I can be set free."

"But your bark is tough as iron." I said,
"Your roots so thick and proud,
Your branches so high and mighty,
They caress the passing clouds."

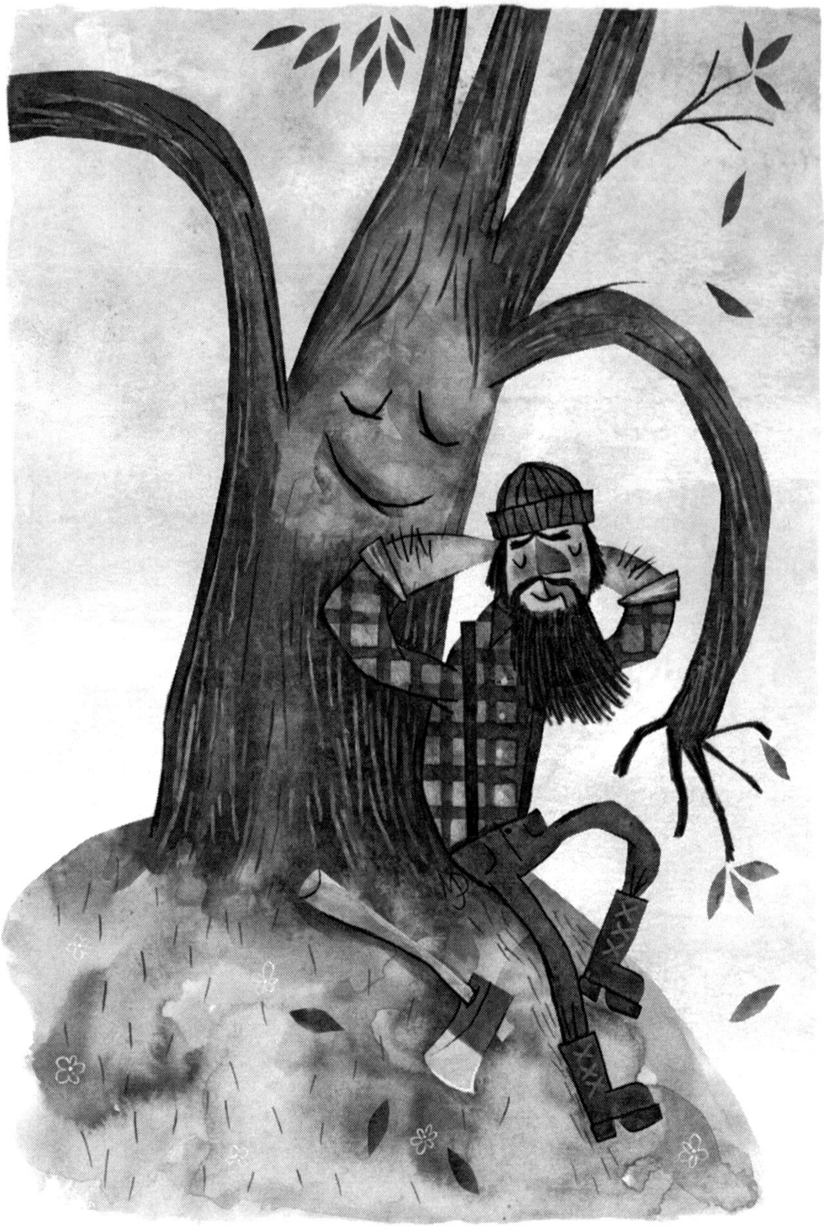

"I will sit beside you everyday,

So you won't feel lonely again,

Because all we need in life sometimes,

Is the company of a friend."

Bagshaw

Bagshaw is an amazing dog,
He can climb ladders and see through fog.
He's really good at howling tunes,
And he loves to dance and play the spoons.
But the thing he does the best of all,
Is to write his name in wee on the wall!

Beddy-byes Land

Let's all go to Beddy-byes land,
To dreams of ships that sail on sand,
And kites that fly without any breeze
Past clouds that look like lumps of cheese.

In Beddy-byes land the animals dance,
While all the children laugh and prance.
The sky is purple, the sun is green,
The sea is yellow with a glittery sheen.

The King, whose name is Dandy Dan,
    Is really quite a lovely man.
    For he has decreed the nicest laws,
Like the banning of household chores.

In Beddy-byes many beards can be found.
There are hairy faces all around.
Some on snakes, some on bees,
Some on twigs which hang from trees.

It really is great in Beddy-byes land,
It makes our world seem rather bland.

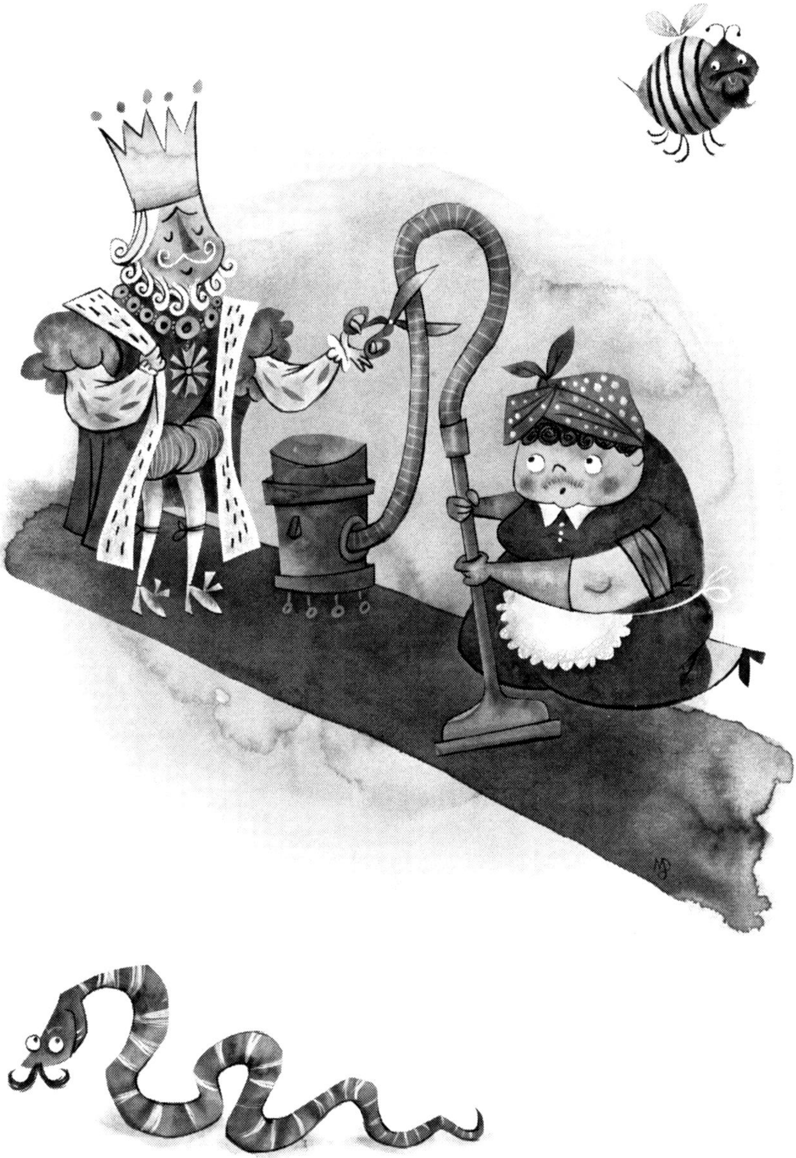

Chuck the Shark

Deep down on the dark sea bed
Lives a shark with a strange shaped head.

It isn't pointy, flat or thin,
It isn't round like an old dustbin.

"So what's it like?" I hear you clamour
Well, it looks just like a workman's hammer.

His name is Chuck and he's real quick
His teeth are sharp, his skin is slick.

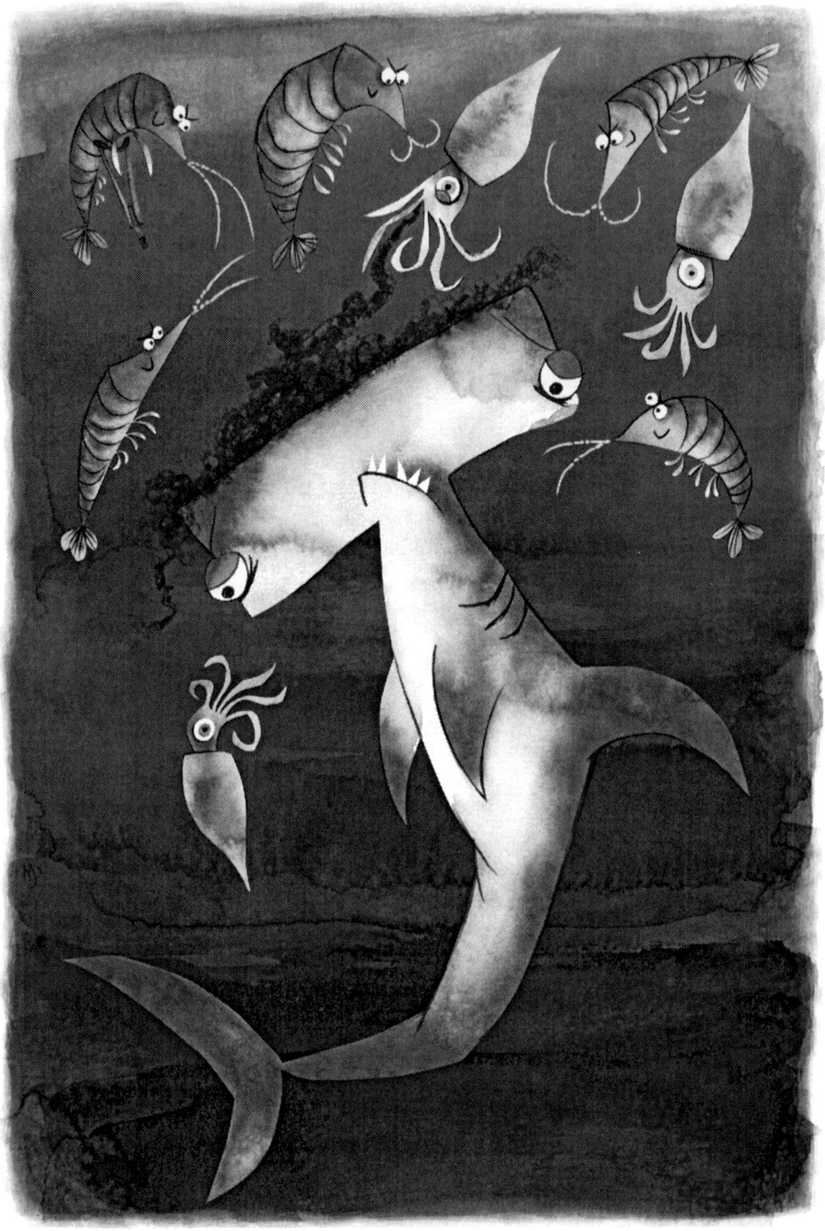

But Chuck is lonely and Chuck is sad,
He has no friends or mum and dad!

And all the squid and all the shrimp,
Including the one with the dodgy limp,

Call Chuck names and mock his features,
Shellfish are the cruellest creatures.

But all that changed one winter's day,
When the sea was rough and the sky was grey,

A small boat that was floating about,
Threw a great big fishing net out,

And all the squid and all the shrimp
including the one with the dodgy limp

Got caught inside, no room to flee,
A fisherman, wanted them all for tea.

They yelled and screamed, they hollered and cried
But nobody came (they had all gone to hide)

Then out of the darkness a shadow appeared
"Chuck's come to save us.' The shellfish cheered.

Using his head he butted and thrashed
Then bit with his teeth till the net had been slashed.

The shellfish were free and swam from the scene,
But stopped to say sorry for being so mean

Now Chuck isn't lonely and Chuck isn't sad.
He has lots of friends which makes him feel glad,

That he has a head that looks like a hammer,
Even though it isn't the height of sea glamour.

Coming Apart

I laughed and my leg fell off today,
I replaced it with a barrel of hay.
Then one of my arms fell to the floor,
I replaced that with an old pine door.

I gave out a cough and my nose flew off,
I replaced that with a soggy old cloth.
But worst of all my bum blew out,
I replaced it with a chimney spout.

So now I'm careful when I laugh or cough,
Because I never know what bits may fall off!

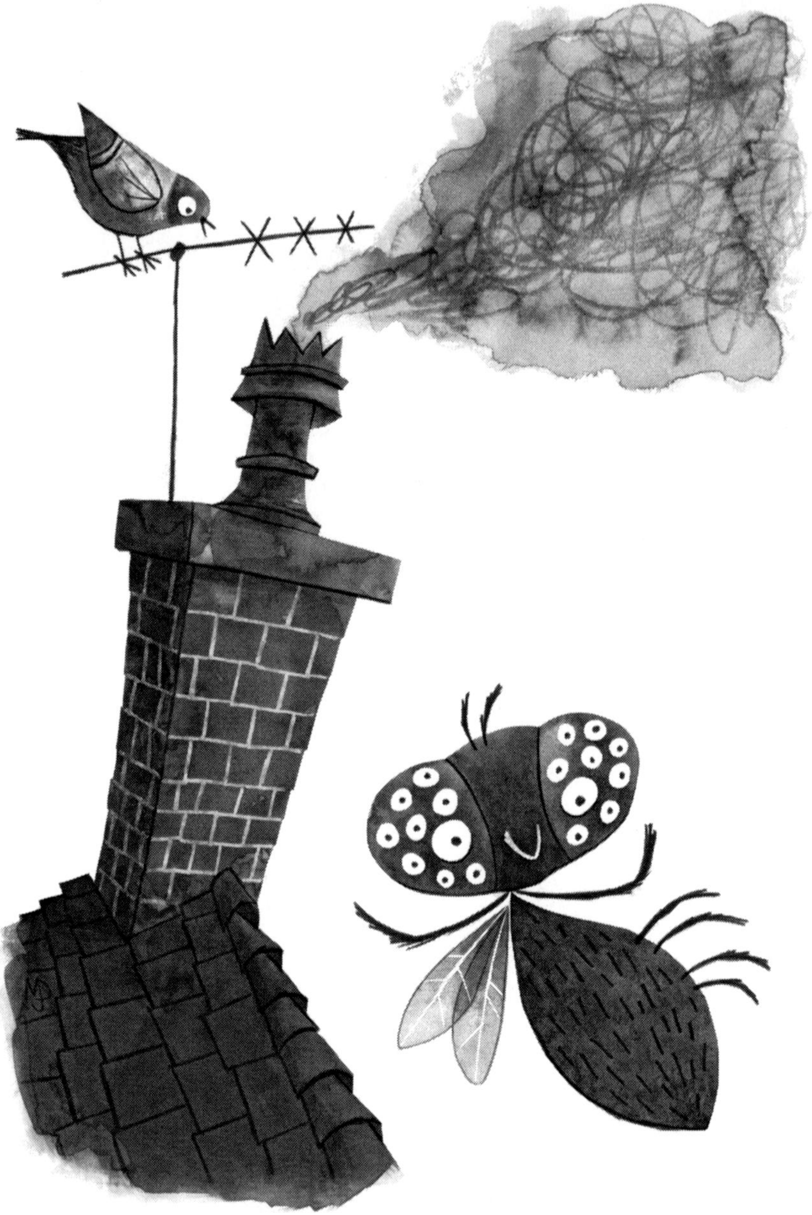

Sid the Fly

Sid was a very daring fly,
There wasn't a thing that he'd not try
Like flying backwards, just for fun,
Or eating cow pats in the sun.

But then one day whilst flying about
He collided with a chimney spout.
Now I don't mean to make you cry
But that was the end of Sid the Fly

the end!

About the Author

Giles was born in East Sussex in 1977 and grew up on the south coast in a little town called Seaford. He neglected his education to pursue a career in music, releasing several EPs and albums with various rock bands and spending a good number of years performing extensively around the UK, including slots at the Glastonbury festival. It was during this time that he first began to develop his skills as a writer, penning lyrics and poetry for use in songs.

In the early 2006 Giles released a collection of lyrics and poems in aid of Leukaemia Research, a charity very dear to his heart, having lost his Mother to the disease when he was six years old.

After the birth of his first son, Elijah and a chance encounter with a collection of nonsense poetry by Shel Silverstein in a charity shop, he was inspired to turn his attention to Children's writing and the pursuit of a career in picture books.

Giles still lives in Seaford with his wife, Michelle and their two sons, Elijah and Sonny. He is currently studying for a BA(Hons) with the Open University.

His hobbies include playing in a rock band called Burnthouse, watching lots of films, forever being disappointed following Crystal Palace FC and lots of running, mainly for public transport!

About the Illustrator

After a few years spent working as a graphic designer Matt felt it was high time he turned his aimless personal doodlings into a new career. With Penguin book covers and various other commissions under his belt Matt can now write "illustrator" under profession when he renews his passport.

He lives in Surrey with his pencils, vast amounts of paper and not enough room for a dog. He can juggle with 3 balls but keeps dropping the fourth.

More of his work can be seen at www.matt-dawson.co.uk.

Also by Rebel Books LLP

An Anthology of Supernatural Teens for young adults. Enter a world of vampires and faeries.

Have you ever wondered what Death would look like if he approached you at a bus stop? Or what would happen if a vampire's chosen victim turned out to be more than they had bargained for?

Rebel Moon is a collection of stories that will whisk you into worlds of vampires, werewolves and witchcraft so prepare yourself for a bumpy ride as sometimes the dead have more of a life than the living and if this book teaches you anything it is to always expect the unexpected!

From the teen witches you wouldn't want to cross in One Witch Down to the dark comedy of Evil 101, this is a book you won't want to put down.

Also by Rebel Books LLP

How can you have a happy ending unless you have a miserable middle?

The Underworld Kingdom is turned upside down when Princess Samantha requests a story with a Happy Ending. Happy Endings are unheard of in a kingdom populated by the deceased. The King and Queen are most alarmed by their daughter's strange behaviour.

Chaos ensues when Death takes a break from his normal career to pursue his passion for poetry and the King decides to pay a visit to the Kingdom Upstairs to track down his rogue employee.

There are many more tales in this collection of short stories from the Underworld Kingdom you won't want to miss.